SERVANT LEADERSHIP

R. PAUL STEVENS
& GERRY SCHOBERG

Harold Shaw Publishers
Wheaton, Illinois

Cover design by John Seid

ISBN 0-87788-755-1

99 98 97 96 95 94 93 92 91 90

10 9 8 7 6 5 4 3 2 1

Contents

How to Use this Discussion Guide

NetWork Discussion Guides are designed for "people on the move." A typical group might use these studies during a lunch break, as part of a fellowship evening in a home, or in a Sunday school class.

Each study is designed to take about 30 minutes to complete. If you have more than 30 minutes, your group can spend valuable time praying and fellowshiping together.

NetWork studies address important contemporary issues from a biblical perspective. Their ultimate goal is to help you put God's Word into practice in your life. To do this, each study includes three segments.

OPENING IT UP

The study begins with a discussion launcher. This might be a short case study, a provocative quote or a problem-posing story intended to spark discussion and draw out personal opinion. Spend about 5 minutes on this opener. It will help you to focus on the theme of the study and will help participants to become involved in the discussion.

THINKING IT THROUGH

This section focuses on a Scripture passage, with 4-6 questions that draw out the facts and the meaning of the passage. These thoughtful questions should take about 15 minutes. Background notes on each passage are part of the Leader's Notes.

MAKING IT HAPPEN

This section brings immediacy and concreteness to the issue, with suggestions for life application. Here, group members are encouraged to ask, "So what? What am I going to do about obeying this Scripture in my home or at my job?" Spend about 10 minutes on this important wrap-up.

Each study also features a Journal Entry for follow-up at home. This is another way to make truth personal and active.

You will find additional suggestions for leading the group and helpful notes on each Scripture passage in the Leader's Notes at the back of the guide.

Introduction

The problem with Christianity is that it's meant to be lived in the world! Following Jesus might not be so difficult if we could retreat to an ideal environment, or confine our beliefs to one or two days a week. But these possibilities are not options for the Christian. The world is the context for practicing true Christianity—every day of the week.

When we bump up against the realities of life it's often difficult to respond Christianly. How am I supposed to love my neighbor when he is trying to put me out of business? How can I value myself and what I do without becoming proud? Where do I find my identity? Can I risk the loss of reputation by being honest and letting my peers know what I am really like? How can I balance the competing agendas of work, family, church, and friends?

By becoming a human being, Jesus showed us that he is concerned about our struggles in this life. He came to redeem and renew this world, not simply to offer us an escape from it. By dying and rising again he demonstrated that he has the power to offer new life. He can transform and bring hope to the most desperate of situations.

These studies will help us focus on the Christian response to everyday challenges of leadership and servanthood. Our prayer is that you may find the liberating life of Jesus Christ in the midst of all your activities, wherever you live those out—in the home, at work, or in the community.

☐ STUDY ONE

MOSES
The Struggle with Inadequacy

Exodus 2:11–25; 3:1–15; 4:1–17

OPENING IT UP

> "Son of Adam," said Aslan. "Are you ready to undo the wrong that you have done to my sweet country of Narnia on the very day of its birth?"
>
> "Well, I don't see what I can do," said Digory. "You see, the Queen ran away and—"
>
> "I asked, are you ready?" said the Lion.
>
> C.S. Lewis, *The Magician's Nephew*

Describe a time when you felt overwhelmed by a task you believed God wanted you to do.

Think about the hardest thing God is asking you to do right now. Write it down and keep it in mind as you go through this study.

THINKING IT THROUGH

1. *Skim Exodus 2:11–25.* What thoughts and feelings do you think Moses might have experienced while tending sheep in the desert?

2. *Read Exodus 3:1–12.* The Scriptures often warn against self-reliance (see Ps. 118:8–9 and Prov. 3:5). In contrast, Moses feels overwhelmed with inadequacy by the task God is giving him (verse 11). What does God offer as an answer to Moses' objection (verse 12)?

3. *Read Exodus 3:13–15.* In the ancient Near East, a person's name was very significant because it was linked to his character or nature. What light does this shed on Moses' question (verse 13)? On God's response (verses 14–15)?

Henri Nouwen records the following incident from the Jewish Talmud in his book *The Wounded Healer:*

> Rabbi Yoshua ben Levi came upon Elijah the prophet while he was standing at the entrance of Rabbi Simeon ben Yohai's cave. . . . He asked Elijah, "When will the Messiah come?"

Elijah replied, "Go and ask him yourself."

"Where is he?"

"Sitting at the gates of the city."

"How shall I know him?"

"He is sitting among the poor covered with wounds. The others unbind all their wounds at the same time and then bind them up again. But he unbinds one at a time and binds it up again, saying to himself, 'Perhaps I shall be needed: if so I must always be ready so as not to delay for a moment.' "

Nouwen continues: "[The minister] is called to be the wounded healer, the one who must look after his own wounds but at the same time be prepared to heal the wounds of others."

How can our wounds and weaknesses help us minister to people?

4. ***Read Exodus 4:1–9.*** What further reason does Moses give for avoiding God's call? How does God respond to this concern?

5. ***Read Exodus 4:13–17.*** When he runs out of excuses, Moses finally but politely asks God to get someone else. After all of Moses' resistance, why do you think God did not assign someone else as Israel's leader?

MAKING IT HAPPEN

In your own vocation or ministry, are you more likely to be self-reliant or to struggle with feelings of inadequacy? Why are both of these responses actually indications of refusing to trust in God?

Do you think Christians today should ask God for evidence of his reality, or is that a sign of weak faith? By what means might God confirm your abilities today?

In what ways do you feel most inadequate? How has God already helped you in one area of weakness?

Journal Entry

Record what you are learning about inadequacy, self-reliance, and trust in God.

☐ STUDY TWO

SIMON
Lust for Power

Acts 8:4–25

OPENING IT UP

> "There was nothing there now except a single Commandment. It ran:
>
> ALL ANIMALS ARE EQUAL
> BUT SOME ANIMALS ARE MORE EQUAL THAN OTHERS
>
> After that it did not seem strange when next day the pigs who were supervising the work of the farm all carried whips in their trotters.
>
> George Orwell, *Animal Farm*

Describe a power-struggle situation that you have recently experienced or observed.

THINKING IT THROUGH

In our study of Moses we explored service that grows out of weakness and powerlessness. In our study of Simon, we focus on a person who lusted for power for the wrong reasons and in the wrong way.

1. *Read Acts 8:4–13.* What was the effect of the spread of the gospel in Samaria?

2. What can you tell about Simon's motives?

3. Why do you think Simon followed the rest of the people in being baptized?

4. *Read Acts 8:14–25.* In the New Testament the possession of the Holy Spirit was the hallmark of true Christianity. By offering the disciples money for the ability to give the Holy Spirit, what genuine aspect of Christianity does Simon show he lacks?

5. J.B. Phillips translates Peter's rebuke of Simon in verse 20, "To hell with you and your money!"—an exact translation of the Greek. Why was Peter so incensed at Simon's request?

MAKING IT HAPPEN

Simon's problem was that he wanted to use the power of God to promote himself. It is not difficult to find similar examples today in religious circles. But how do you see the same thing occurring in your workplace or in other settings?

The exercise of power over people is not always as demonstrative and aggressive as it was in Simon's case. What are some of the more subtle ways power is misused in our society?

How would you structure a group of people (whether in the workplace, church, or other organization) to minimize the misuse of power?

> You are not free as a Christian to compete for power in this world or in the church for your own use. But you are free to seek to promote God's Kingdom in the hearts of men and to establish the Church of Jesus in this world . . . The key to the whole issue is: are you using deference, courtesy, and public relations to get others to accede power to you for your sake, or are you using these things to create a new and wider sphere of influence for God in this world? . . . Servant leadership is the all-important checkpoint that bridles demonic power. As long as we follow Christ, we are safe! It is impossible to live out Christian servanthood and wield the mace of abusive power. He who tries to rule from the throne of Christ is a usurper, and not a servant (Calvin Miller, *Leadership*).

Journal Entry

In what ways are you tempted to lust for power? How can you deal with this?

☐ STUDY THREE

THE SERVANT
Discovering Our Identity in God

Isaiah 42:1–9

OPENING IT UP

Jill accepted a job as administrative assistant to a Christian politician. She brought to the task both superb administrative skills and idealism. This job was definitely a move up and it was good for her self-image—except for the people she had to work with. The office secretary, Melinda, was hired by the politician out of pity; she had just gone through a divorce and needed the work desperately. Jill found her incompetent and grew weary as Melinda kept dissolving into tears in the presence of important guests. Jill had to cover for her time and again. But when her boss asked Jill to approve an expense voucher for his wife's private dinner party, Jill lost something crucial: respect for her employer. She began to wonder who she was serving, and whether being everyone's servant was really being a servant of God.

Think about a situation you have been in where serving God seemed to run contrary to what others wanted you to do to serve them.

THINKING IT THROUGH

1. *Read Isaiah 42:1–9.* This is the first of four "Servant Songs" in the Book of Isaiah (the others are 49:1–7; 50:4–9, and 52:13–53:12). While these songs were ultimately fulfilled in Jesus, they are meant to speak of Israel and of Christians today as well. The first song describes the servant's identity. What actions of God assure the servant that he has not taken the task of ministry on himself (verse 1)?

2. The biblical understanding of justice encompasses *both* justice between people in society *and* right relationship with God. In this poem how is the servant's ministry of bringing justice portrayed?

3. *Reread verse 7.* Similar words in Isaiah 61:1–2 were quoted by Jesus as the Father's agenda for his own ministry (Luke 4:18–19). What clues are there in the whole poem which would help you form a philosophy of service which includes both social action and evangelism?

4. Review the whole song again. Note what *promises* of God would keep the servant going in hard times.

5. Many Christian servants become very discouraged because they feel they are expected to do the wishes of those they serve. Their service does not spring from the freedom of their own hearts but from conformity to human demands or expectations. What have you learned from this poem that will help you serve people with a free spirit *because* you serve God?

MAKING IT HAPPEN

Some of the people you are called to serve are like broken reeds ready to snap or smoldering wicks down to their last flicker. In the opening case study Melinda was such a person. Name some of these people in your own life and describe how you are called to serve them.

In what other way(s) do you, or could you, seek to bring justice into the world as an expression of service to God?

Why is it so important for a servant to find his or her identity in relation to God rather than the task? Explain how this proves to be true in your own life.

WHO AM I?

Who am I? They often tell me
I stepped from my cell's confinement
Calmly, cheerfully, firmly,
Like a squire from his country-house.
Who am I? They often tell me
I used to speak to my warders
Freely and friendly and clearly,
As though it were mine to command.
Who am I? They also tell me
I bore the days of misfortune
Equably, smilingly, proudly,
Like one accustomed to win.
Am I then really all that which other men tell of?
Or am I only what I myself know of myself?
Restless and longing and sick, like a bird in a cage,
Struggling for breath, as though bands were compressing
  my throat,
Yearning for colours, for flowers, for the voices of birds,
Thirsting for words of kindness, for neighbourliness,
Tossing in expectation of great events,
Powerlessly trembling for friends at an infinite distance,
Weary and empty at praying, at thinking, at making,
Faint, and ready to say farewell to it all?

Who am I? This or the other?
Am I one person to-day and to-morrow another?
Am I both at once? A hypocrite before others,
And before myself a contemptibly woebegone weakling?
Or is something within me still like a beaten army,
Fleeing in disorder from victory already achieved?

Who am I? they mock me, these lonely questions of mine,
Whoever I am, Thou knowest, O God, I am thine!

(Dietrich Bonhoeffer, *Letters and Papers from Prison*).

Journal Entry

How would you answer the question: "Who am I?"

☐ STUDY FOUR

ELI

The Toxic Mix of Work, Marriage, and Family

1 Samuel 2:12–36

OPENING IT UP

Robert has been asked to accept a transfer to a distant city as sales manager of a large retail outlet. It is the promotion of his dreams. But his children, in sensitive teen years, do not want to move. Robert knows that the new job will make demands on his evenings and weekends; family life could suffer. His wife, Jillian, feels caught in the middle in several ways.

Jillian has been a homemaker and volunteer in the church for eleven years. But just as Robert was considering his offer, Jillian was asked by the official board of her church to accept a half-time paid position as Director of Children's Ministries. It would mean evening courses in the local theological school, less time with the children, and not moving.

What are the factors that should influence Robert's and Jillian's decision?

THINKING IT THROUGH

1. *Read 1 Samuel 2:12–26.* What was so wicked about what Eli's sons were doing?

2. Why had Eli not fulfilled his responsibility for disciplining his sons by his rebuke in verses 22–25?

3. *Read 1 Samuel 2:27–36.* Although Eli may have been lacking in discernment (1 Sam. 1:12–17), for what wickedness specifically does the man of God hold Eli responsible?

4. When it comes to rearing his own children, Samuel does not seem to be any more successful than Eli (1 Sam. 8:1–5). Why do you think people in ministry and leadership frequently neglect (often unintentionally) to meet the needs of their immediate family members?

5. The passage for this study has said nothing about spouses, yet one's marriage partner is just as easily hurt from neglect as children are. How can you and your spouse (if you are married or intend to marry) encourage and strengthen each other in your respective vocations and family roles?

Over the last twenty or thirty years psychologists have been saying that the basic unit of society is the individual rather than the family. In the gospel of self-fulfillment any commitment or loyalty may be broken if it stands in the way of someone's fulfillment. In his book *New Rules: Searching for Self-Fulfillment in a World Turned Upside Down*, Daniel Yankelovich exposes this "me-first" outlook on life whose tenets are "... live for the moment, regard the self as a sacred object, be more self-assertive, express all feelings, hold nothing back." Whether subtle or obvious it is clear that this kind of philosophy has permeated Western society, including the church. Yankelovich goes on to argue that although self-fulfillment may be good, it is not the most important thing. He says that what we need is an "*ethic of commitment* which shifts the axis away from the self ... toward connectedness with the world" (Daniel Yankelovich, *New Rules: Searching for Self-Fulfillment in a World Turned Upside Down*).

MAKING IT HAPPEN

Describe a hard decision you have faced regarding vocation and family. How would you cope differently with this decision in the light of this study?

In what specific ways do the challenges of friendship, marriage, or family call for a deeper spirituality in your life?

Journal Entry

Recall your own family upbringing. What were some of the positive dimensions of spiritual formation which you learned at home?

☐ Study Five

ELIJAH
The Peril of Individualism

1 Kings 19:1–21

OPENING IT UP

> Frequently the approach to overcoming unfruitful ministry and burnout is to try new programs and new activities. . . .
>
> Activism makes service, not God, the goal of the Christian life. Mature Christians are seen as those who are busy doing things for God. The best churches are the ones that offer the most programs and activities. Every night of the week there are opportunities for Bible study, choir, aerobic exercise, visitation, supper clubs, scouting, sports, and a thousand other things. . . .
>
> How do we escape? First by discovering that our activistic service for God is only another expression of worldliness. We need God, not more ministries. We need the power of the Spirit, not more programs. We need to find out what it really means to serve God (Stephen D. Eyre, *Defeating the Dragons of the World).*

Think about the last six months of your life. Have you been able to serve God responsibly, or is your life characterized by stressful activism?

THINKING IT THROUGH

1. ***Read 1 Kings 19:1–9a.*** As Elijah was fleeing from Jezebel, who had sworn to kill him, what do you think his feelings were toward God?

2. This chapter follows immediately after the episode on Mount Carmel (1 Kings 18:16ff) where Elijah won a mighty victory over the false god Baal and his prophets. Why would someone like Elijah be susceptible to depression, discouragement, and even a death-wish (19:4) after such a great victory?

3. ***Read 1 Kings 19:9b–18.*** Twice in this section God asks Elijah why he has come to Horeb (verses 9, 13). In response, how does Elijah describe the condition of Israel, and how does he perceive his own situation?

4. There are several similarities between Elijah in this chapter and Moses at Mt. Sinai: Both of them had an experience lasting "forty days and forty nights" (verse 8; Exod. 24:18); both went to Horeb (the same as Mt. Sinai); and both were concerned with the covenant between God and Israel (verses 10, 14; Exod. 19:3–6). What do you think Elijah was expecting from God?

5. How does God correct, challenge, and encourage Elijah (verses 11–13, 15–18)?

6. *Read 1 Kings 19:19–21.* This passage tells how Elisha became Elijah's attendant. How does this incident demonstrate a change in Elijah's perception of his ministry?

MAKING IT HAPPEN

How have you seen Elijah's experience of success followed by temptation or depression in yourself or someone you work with?

How can you encourage or strengthen someone who is experiencing this kind of depression?

Fear of burnout can keep people from wholehearted involvement. What is the biblical and spiritual remedy for this fear?

> Christians are burning out in great numbers because they've not discovered the way to stay alive in the resources of the Spirit of Christ rather than through their own energy.
>
> Some people feel a lack of enough strength and energy to do all they're called to do. Usually that means they're attempting to do some things God hasn't called them to do. As I understand it, our will, done in our own strength, is humanism. Christ's will, done in our own strength, is religion. And his will, done by his power, is the abundant life. And there's a great difference (Lloyd John Ogilvie, "Keeping the Drive Alive," *Leadership*, Summer 1989).

Journal Entry

What can you do to avoid unnecessary emotional and spiritual exhaustion?

☐ STUDY SIX

THE PHARISEE AND THE PUBLICAN

Comparing Ourselves

Luke 18:9–14

OPENING IT UP

In our competitive Western society we often compare ourselves with others—in sports, business, academics, ministry, and even spirituality.

Bill is a mid-level executive whose annual review shows that he fails to take initiative as well as his peers. He feels inferior.

Sue always felt she was a superior mother to the others in the mom's drop-in center until her own world caved in: her teen-age daughter ran away for a few days.

Jeremy pastors an inner-city church that has an outstanding ministry to the many ethnic groups in the area in spite of constantly losing members to the suburbs. But he dreads going to ministerial meetings where his peers report substantial growth and progress.

It is easy for Bill, Sue, and Jeremy to allow their self-images to be determined by how they compare with others, or how others evaluate them.

In what ways have you been tempted to think less of yourself by comparing yourself unfavorably with others?

Few of us would say out loud that we think we are superior, but we may think it. How, if at all, have these thoughts affected your well-being?

THINKING IT THROUGH

The Pharisees were convinced that Israel's problems resulted from the people's failure to keep God's law. Although their preoccupation with fulfilling the written letter became a merit-based system and an end in itself, their enthusiasm made Pharisaism the most influential power in Judaism in Jesus' day.

In contrast, tax collectors (Jews who collected taxes from their countrymen for the Romans) were despised and considered to be traitors to Israel. They regularly abused the system by demanding extra for themselves. Furthermore, because their work brought them into continual contact with Gentiles and required them to work on the Sabbath, they were ceremonially unclean, and therefore unfit to enter the temple or to eat with another Jew.

1. *Read Luke 18:9–14.* How would Jesus' hearers have responded to this parable?

2. Verse 11 can be translated two different ways: "The Pharisee stood up and prayed *about* himself," or "The Pharisee stood up and prayed *to* himself." Is there any practical difference between the two? Why or why not?

3. Elsewhere in the New Testament we are told that the kinds of people mentioned in the Pharisee's prayer will not inherit the kingdom of God (Gal 5:19–21). And indeed, all that the Pharisee prays sounds proper. What then is wrong with his prayer?

4. What brought the tax collector justification?

> It is grace we need, and not sin, to make and keep us humble. The heaviest-laden branches always bow the lowest. The greatest flow of water makes the deepest river-bed. The nearer the soul comes to God, the more His majestic presence makes it feel its littleness. It is this alone that makes it possible for each to count others better than himself. Jesus Christ, the Holy One of God, is our example of humility: knowing that the Father had given all things into His hands, and that He was come from God and went to God, He washed the disciples' feet. It is the divine presence, the consciousness of divine life and the divine love in us, that will make us humble (Andrew Murray, *Like Christ*).

5. What is the main difference between the spirituality of the Pharisee and the tax collector?

6. Why would it be inappropriate to thank God that you are not like this Pharisee?

MAKING IT HAPPEN

A psychologist would probably assess that the Pharisee had a good self-image and a healthy personality. He eagerly sought to do good and to be good. On the other hand, the tax collector appears to have had a poor self-image because he was down on himself. Do you agree with this assessment? Why or why not?

Do you agree that self-hatred can be the cloak of pride turned inside out—just another way of putting ourselves in the center?

According to this parable, where does true humility come from? In what ways will this true humility improve your relationship with others?

> Humility does not rest, in final count, upon bafflement and discouragement and self-disgust at our shabby lives, a brow-beaten, dog-slinking attitude. It rests upon the disclosure of the consummate wonder of God, upon finding that only God counts, that all our own self-originated intentions are works of straw. And so in lowly humility we must stick close to the Root and count our own powers as nothing except as they are enslaved in His power (Thomas Kelly, *A Testament of Devotion).*

Journal Entry

Reflect on a realistic self-appraisal, based on who you are in Christ. (Reject the temptation to base your self-appraisal on a comparison with other people!)

☐ Study Seven

PAUL
The Servant Leader

2 Corinthians 3:7–4:12

OPENING IT UP

The Skin Horse had lived longer in the nursery than any of the others. He was so old that his brown coat was bald in patches and showed the seams underneath, and most of the hairs in his tail had been pulled out to string bead necklaces. He was wise, for he had seen a long succession of mechanical toys arrive to boast and swagger, and by-and-by break their mainsprings and pass away, and he knew that they were only toys, and would never turn into anything else. . . .

"What is real?" asked the Rabbit one day, when they were lying side by side near the nursery fender, before Nana came to tidy the room. "Does it mean having things that buzz inside you and a stick out handle?"

"Real isn't how you are made," said the Skin Horse. "It's a thing that happens to you. When a child loves you for a long, long time, not just to play with, but REALLY loves you, then you become Real."

"Does it hurt?" asked the Rabbit.

"Sometimes," said the Skin Horse, for he was always truthful. "When you are Real you don't mind being hurt."

"Does it happen all at once, like being wound up," he asked, "or bit by bit?"

> "It doesn't happen all at once," said the Skin Horse. "You become. It takes a long time. That's why it doesn't often happen to people who break easily, or have sharp edges, or who have to be carefully kept. Generally, by the time you are Real, most of your hair has been loved off, and your eyes drop out and you get loose in the joints and very shabby. But these things don't matter at all, because once you are Real you can't be ugly, except to people who don't understand" (Margery Williams, *The Velveteen Rabbit*).

Leaders often feel that if people knew their weaknesses and struggles, they would lose credibility. When have you had similar thoughts?

THINKING IT THROUGH

In 1 Corinthians we look inside a first-century church. But in 2 Corinthians we get a look inside a first-century Christian, the apostle Paul. It is truth strained through personality, incarnational ministry.

1. *Read 2 Corinthians 4:1–6.* Why is Paul encouraged not to lose heart in his ministry (verse 1)?

2. What qualities characterized Paul's ministry (verses 2, 5)?

3. What was the condition of those to whom he ministered (verses 3–4)? What hope is expressed for this condition in verse 6?

4. *Read 2 Corinthians 4:7–12.* Why does God put his treasure in jars of clay?

5. What contrasts are expressed in verses 8–12?

MAKING IT HAPPEN

What have you learned from this study about ministry and leadership?

If God ministers through our weakness and humanity, and not merely "in spite of us," what do you now understand to be the relationship of personal spirituality and our ministry to others?

> We are like Kodachrome transparencies: no image is seen by looking directly at it, but only by looking through it, provided there is light on the other side. It seems to us that it should be as we hide ourselves that Christ is most revealed, that Christ should be hidden by our self-revelation. But that is the Old Covenant with its fading glory, condemnation and death-dealing impact. New Covenant ministry is paradoxically this: as I look at Christ, and as I reveal myself, it is not I who am revealed but Christ. This is unself-conscious self-consciousness, the unselfing of the self. It makes all Christian ministry inevitably and inescapably personal.—R. Paul Stevens

Journal Entry

Reflect on the actual weaknesses you have which, by God's grace, can become a source and center of ministry to others.

☐ STUDY EIGHT

THE BLESSED PERSON

Christianity in the World

Matthew 5:1–16

OPENING IT UP

However small our part may be, we cannot opt out of seeking to create better social structures, which guarantee justice in legislation and law enforcement, the freedom and dignity of the individual, civil rights for minorities, and the abolition of social and racial discrimination. We should neither despise these things nor avoid our responsibility for them. They are part of God's purpose for his people. Whenever Christians are conscientious citizens, they are acting like salt in the community. As Sir Frederick Catherwood put it . . . "To try to improve society is not worldliness but love. To wash your hands of society is not love but worldliness" (John R.W. Stott, *Christian Counter-Culture*).

THINKING IT THROUGH

1. *Read Matthew 5:1–12.* The subjects of the first two beatitudes—the "poor in spirit" and "those who mourn"—suggest a reference is being made back to Isaiah 61:1–2 (a description of Jesus' future ministry):

> The Spirit of the Sovereign LORD is on me,
> because the LORD has anointed me
> to preach good news to the poor.
> He has sent me to bind up the brokenhearted,
> to proclaim freedom for the captives
> and release from darkness for the prisoners,
> to proclaim the year of the LORD's favor
> and the day of vengeance of our God,
> to comfort all who mourn . . .

In what ways is Jesus' ministry reflected in the Beatitudes?

2. In the Old Testament the poor were often taken advantage of by the rich and powerful. They became the social and religious outcasts of society. Consequently, the only hope they had was to place all their trust in God. How would you recognize the quality of "poor in spirit" in someone today?

3. Consider all of the qualities of those Jesus calls blessed. Do you think he is referring to eight different categories of people or to eight different characteristics of one people? Explain.

4. Many have been confused over whether the Beatitudes are ethical entrance requirements to the kingdom of God or a description of what life in the kingdom will be like in the future, but not applicable today. However, neither of these represent the true picture. Jesus did not preach a new legalism, but he did expect his followers to live this way now. We should understand the beatitudes as an announcement which produces what it announces.

In what way(s) is Jesus' message both good news of God's free grace and a description of appropriate lifestyle for Christians?

5. *Read Matthew 5:13–16.* Jesus shifts from describing the character and future of his disciples to setting forth the disciples' mission in the world. What qualities of salt and light do you think Jesus had in mind in these verses?

6. In Matthew 6:1 Jesus says, "Be careful not to do your acts of righteousness before men, to be seen by them," but here he says to "let your light shine before men that they may see your good deeds. . . ." How do you reconcile these two statements?

MAKING IT HAPPEN

How can you ensure that the way you follow Jesus is not hidden, but rather makes you to be salt and light in the world?

In what way do you feel called to live out the Beatitudes in your sphere of work or service?

In what specific ways have you found that godliness leads to service and that service in the world leads to godliness?

As the artist discovers that there is a direct relationship between the inner and outer forms of material, so we discover that creativity in our own lives has a direct relationship to creativity in the world. We can never be in the world only as its benefactors. This does not make for authentic relationship. All that we genuinely do is very personal and calls into being our own personality. The covenant of the Church to call forth gifts is extended to the whole of mankind. I say to the world, "I will be an instrument of God in the continuing act of creation," and the world fulfills in me its side of the covenant. It brings forth in me the new creation (Elizabeth O'Connor *Eighth Day of Creation).*

Journal Entry

How are you called to be salt and light in society? Where in the world are you for God?

Leader's Notes

Study One

Question 1. C.S. Lewis said he often felt spiritually weak when far from home in lonely hotel rooms. Moses could have felt disoriented and detached from his physical and spiritual roots in this remote wilderness setting. He may have been reflecting on his home and his people.

Question 3. Asking about the "name" of God was a question about God's revealed nature, since to the Semites the name disclosed the person. Note how verses 13-15 pull together the past, present, and future in God's relationship to his people.

Study Two

Question 4. "At first each step taken by the Samaritans is paralleled by a similar step taken by Simon: they turn from magic to Philip, so does he; they believe Philip, so does he; they are baptized by Philip, so is he. But then their paths diverge—*they* receive the Spirit, whereas Simon receives only a curse. This contrast is the climax of the whole incident—the Samaritans receive the Spirit, which indicates that they have come to genuine faith, but Simon continues to see and be interested in only the external" (James Dunn, *Baptism in the Holy Spirit*, Philadelphia: Westminster Press, 1970).

Question 5. Richard Foster comments on this passage: "The sin of Simon . . . was to try to use the Power of God for his own ends. This is the sign of all false religion, but it is exactly this mentality that has come over so much of Christianity in our day" (*Money, Sex & Power*, San Francisco: Harper & Row, 1985).

Study Three

Question 2. "The biblical concept of justice is much different and even more foreign to modern Americans. Far from being impartial, it reflects special concern for protecting vulnerable people from victimization by the powerful. Justice is so closely linked with the concepts of righteousness and peace that the three often merge. It brings judgment on the wrongdoer but also works to restore the victim, the offender and the community. And most important, it stems not from the image of a minor Greek goddess (Justicia), but from the character of the one true God, Jehovah" (Daniel W. Van-Ness, *Crime and Its Victims*, Downers Grove, Ill.: InterVarsity Press, 1986).

Question 3. "Jesus went on to demonstrate in His ministry a deep compassion for the suffering and the forgotten. He fed the hungry, healed the lame, gave sight to the blind. He was concerned not only with saving man from hell in the next world but delivering him from the hellishness of this one. Thus, the Son reflected the Father's passion for mercy and justice" (Charles Colson, *Loving God*, Grand Rapids, Mich.: Zondervan Publishing, 1983).

Study Four

Question 1. Eli's sons were taking advantage of their trusted position to satisfy their own lusts. See Leviticus 7:22–25 regarding prohibitions for eating the fat of sacrificial animals.

Question 2. Leviticus 7:25 states that any who violate God's offerings should be "cut off from his people." No wonder it was difficult for Eli to confront his sons' sins. But because he didn't, they ruined their own lives and the lives of many others.

Study Five

Question 2. The distance Elijah traveled was over 200 miles. Physically, he was drained and vulnerable. He felt very alone, not realizing that 7,000 others in Israel were still faithful to God. Elijah illustrates that "we are never closer to defeat than in our moments of greatest victory."

Question 5. God provided Elijah with food, shelter, and an "audiovisual display." Then he commanded action, assuring Elijah of resources he never knew about.

Study Six

Question 1. When reading this parable today, we quite readily identify ourselves with the piety of the tax collector and shun the Pharisee as a hypocrite. (The very word "Pharisee" now has the connotation of hypocrisy.) But this was not so in Jesus' day. Pharisaism was the most respected religious power at that time, while tax collectors were despised. Jesus' hearers would have been astounded by this parable.

Question 3. The Pharisee wasn't praying to God—he was announcing his greatness to anyone within hearing distance.

Question 4. The tax collector recognized his sin and begged for mercy—the only basis for justification.

Study Seven

Question 4. Paul's focus is not on the fragile container, but on its contents—God's power. Knowing that the power is God's, not ours, keeps us from pride.

Question 5. "Paul reminds us that though we may be at the end of our rope, we are never at the end of hope . . . Because Christ won victory over death, we have eternal life. All our risks, humiliations, and trials are opportunities to demonstrate Christ's power and presence in us" (*Life Application Bible,* Wheaton, Ill.: Tyndale House, 1988).

Study Eight

Question 3. ". . . the beatitudes are Christ's own specification of what every Christian ought to be. All these qualities are to characterize all his followers" (John R.W. Stott, *Christian Counter-Culture,* Downers Grove, Ill.: InterVarsity, 1979).

Question 6. The key is in the motive—not doing good deeds "to be seen by them" but "that they may praise your Father in heaven."

Bibliography

Barclay, William. *The Gospel of Matthew, vol. I.* Edinburgh: St. Andrew Press, 1958.

Bonhoeffer, Dietrich. *Letters and Papers from Prison.* London: Fontana, 1959.

Colson, Charles. *Loving God.* Grand Rapids, Mich.: Zondervan, 1983.

Dumbrell, William J. *Covenant and Creation: An Old Testament Covenantal Theology.* Exeter, Devon: Paternoster Press, 1984.

Dunn, James. *Baptism in the Holy Spirit.* Philadelphia: Westminster Press, 1970.

Eyre, Stephen D. *Defeating the Dragons of the World.* Downers Grove, Ill.: InterVarsity Press, 1987.

Foster, Richard. *Money, Sex & Power.* San Francisco: Harper & Row, 1985.

Guelich, Robert. *The Sermon on the Mount: A Foundation for Understanding.* Waco, Tex.: Word, Inc., 1982.

Hart, Archibald D. *Theology, News and Notes,* Fuller Theological Seminary, March 1984.

Kelly, Thomas. *A Testament of Devotion.* New York: Harper, 1941.

Kidner, Derek. *The Proverbs: An Introduction and Commentary,* Tyndale Old Testament Commentary Series. Downers Grove, Ill.: InterVarsity Press, 1964.

Lewis, C.S. *The Magician's Nephew.* New York: Macmillan, 1955.

Life Application Bible. Wheaton, Ill.: Tyndale House, 1988.

Miller, Calvin. *Leadership.* Colorado Springs: NavPress, 1987.

Moltmann, Jurgen. *The Power of the Powerless,* trans. M. Kohl. London: SCM Press, 1983.

Mouw, Richard J. *Called to Holy Worldliness.* Philadelphia: Fortress Press, 1980.

Murray, Andrew. *Like Christ.* Springdale, Penn.: Whitaker House, 1983.

Nouwen, Henri. *The Wounded Healer.* Garden City, N.Y.: Image Books, 1979.

O'Connor, Elizabeth. *Eighth Day of Creation.* Waco, Tex.: Word, Inc., 1971.

Ogilvie, Lloyd John. "Keeping the Drive Alive," in *Leadership,* Summer 1989, Wheaton, Ill.: Christianity Today, Inc., 1987.

Orwell, George. *Animal Farm.* New York: Harcourt, Brace, Jovanovich, 1954.

Stevens, R. Paul. "The Price of Leadership," *His,* Downers Grove, Ill.: InterVarsity Press, January, 1974.

Stott, John R.W. *Christian Counter-Culture.* Downers Grove, Ill.: InterVarsity Press, 1979.

Toffler, Alvin. *The Third Wave.* New York: Bantam Books, 1980.

VanNess, Daniel W. *Crime and Its Victims.* Downers Grove, Ill.: InterVarsity Press, 1986.

Williams, Margery. *The Velveteen Rabbit.* New York: Avon Books, 1975.

Yankelovich, Daniel. *New Rules: Searching for Self-Fulfillment in a World Turned Upside Down.* New York: Bantan Books, 1982.